Told on the Pagoda:
Tales of Burmah
Mabel Mary Agnes
Cosgrove Chan-Toon

Told on the Pagoda: Tales of Burmah
Copyright 2014 © Jiahu Books
First Published in Great Britain in 2014 by Jiahu Books – part of Richardson-Prachai Solutions Ltd, Egerton Gate, Milton Keynes, MK5 7HH
ISBN: 978-1-78435-067-3
Conditions of sale
All rights reserved. You must not circulate this book in any other binding or cover and you must impose the same condition on any acquirer.
A CIP catalogue record for this book is available from the British Library.
Visit us at: **jiahubooks.co.uk**

THE WOMAN, THE MAN AND THE NĀT	5
A FABLE	11
THE STOLEN TREASURE	17
THE VIGIL OF MAH MAY	27
THE PETITION TO THE KING	36
THE PRIEST'S PETITION	41
THE COMMAND OF THE KING	49

THE WOMAN, THE MAN AND THE NĀT.

IN every large tree there lives a Nāt, and it is a custom very strictly adhered to that before any tree can be touched the permission of the spirit must be asked and obtained.

Now a woodman cut down a tree one day without giving the Nāt who resided in it the slightest warning, a proceeding which infuriated the spirit exceedingly, and he determined to be revenged; so, taking upon himself without delay the exact form and likeness of the woodman, he gathered up a bundle of sticks and went in advance of him to his home, in the brief warm gloom that precedes the fall of night. When he reached the hut, that was as bare as a hermit's cell, thatched with dunni leaves, and situated in one of the deepest recesses of the dense sylvan growth, he placed the wood outside and went within. An oil lamp stood on the wooden ledge of the entrance and threw a faint light on all around. The wife of the woodcutter was busy boiling the evening rice, a baby slept in its box-like cradle slung from a beam in the roof; a little boy of five or six sat cutting plaintain leaves.

The Nāt greeted the woman; she answered him cheerily. Then he squatted down on a piece of matting.

The rice being ready, the wife put it out on the plaintain leaves, giving one to her supposed husband, one to the boy, and keeping the other for herself. They ate together, and when they had finished drank some water from the chatty standing near. Then they sat and smoked, and talked together of the many little trifling events which went to make up their world. The woman cleared away the remains of their meal, and took out some betel chews and commenced to roll them, while the child slept behind the purdah. About half an hour passed away thus, when lo! on the stillness broke the voice of the woodman calling to his wife that he was coming, saying that he had been delayed.

The woman heard in bewildered astonishment, then turned to the Nāt, who apparently had not heeded the call, and asked him if she dreamt.

Then rising, she peered out into the gloom, just faintly relieved by the rays of a young moon, and beheld the form of a woodcutter coming between the trees, identically the same in figure and face as her husband who was there beside her. The new-comer called her by her name again, bidding her prepare something for him to eat, as he was tired and hungry.

He threw the wood down that he carried, and entered, but staggered back on seeing his counterpart squatting, quite at home, on the ground. The woman looked from one to the other, and knew not what to do or think.

There was silence for a few moments. Then he who had come last asked, when he had sufficiently recovered himself to speak

"Who is this man who bears so strange a likeness to me?"

"I am the husband of this woman," answered the Nāt calmly, not even removing his green-leaf cigar from between his lips.

"That cannot be," exclaimed the other indignantly, "because I am he."

The Nāt shook his head, and went on smoking.

The woodcutter, mad with anger and astonishment, turned excitedly to his wife, and cried—

"Do you not know me, I, your husband, who left you only this morning? Do you not know me, or do you forget so soon, that you accept a stranger in my place?"

The woman looked from one to the other, and examined each carefully, and was more puzzled than ever.

"Oh, wife, do you not know me, do you not know me?" moaned the woodman in a grief-stricken voice.

The woman wrung her hands as she answered—

"I don't know if you are my husband; you are both so much alike that I cannot tell." Then she broke down and wept.

And the Nāt hearing, smiled where he sat in the shadows.

After awhile the woman dried her tears, smoothed back her heavy masses of black hair, and asked what was to be done.

They neither of them answered. Then she said, "Let us go and seek Manoo, and abide by what he says."

Manoo was a very learned judge, who had been appointed, while still quite young, Chief Justice of the King's Court, and was renowned for the wise and prudent judgments that he invariably pronounced.

The Nāt objected to the proposition. Secretly he feared that Manoo might perhaps guess his identity; but the woodman assented eagerly to his wife's idea, and between them they overcame the other's dislike, and the three started without delay, going through the forest between the silvered line of palm-trees; the fire-flies danced before them, and the bats flitted by like ghosts in the warm darkness. All that night and part of the next they travelled, until they reached the Court of Manoo, which was a large white building, supported by chunamed pillars, and with many carved doors.

The judge himself, magnificently arrayed, sat upon a raised couch, that was covered with scarlet satin, richly embroidered, and with a heavy fringe of gold and jewels edging it.

The woman, the Nāt, and the woodman, leaving their shoes at the gates, entered, and, seating themselves at a respectful distance on separate pieces of matting, told their tale.

The judge listened in silence to the end; then he asked the woman if her husband had any particular mark on him by which she could distinguish him.

Her face lightened as she answered that he had a black mark on his back and a red scar on his knee. Then Manoo had both men examined carefully, but found that each had the same marks in the same places.

The woman became more hopelessly bewildered than ever, and knew not what to make of the extraordinary circumstance; while the judge found himself in a position of considerable difficulty.

He saw that he would have to consider the matter carefully for some time; so he bade them go, and return on the following day at the same hour.

Then he went home to his house, which was a gift from his royal master, and was situated on a rocky promontory, with the sea rolling up almost to the entrance. Seating himself alone in his study—the windows of which looked out over the water to where a rich sunset glowed westward, edging the waves with freckled lustre, and throwing purple, amber, and azure lights over the white-crested waves—he became absorbed in deep thought, as a result of which he came to a solution of the matter. On the next day, therefore, when his three strange applicants presented themselves before him, he had a wooden wheel brought into the room and placed in the middle of the floor, saying at the same time—

"The man who shall go through the hole in that wheel will be a wonderful man, and will be recognised as the real husband of this woman."

On hearing which the woodman protested, saying that it was impossible for any human being to go through so small a space, that it was only large enough to admit of an arm; and he grumbled greatly, saying that the test was very unfair.

But Manoo bade him be patient and silent yet awhile. Then he turned to the Nāt, and asked him what he thought. The Nāt, who was laughing inwardly, at once replied that he could perform the task that the woodcutter deemed impossible. The judge smiled a little complacently as he bade him do it.

The Nāt immediately went to and fro through the hole with the greatest ease, the woman looking on in speechless amaze.

Then said Manoo—

"I suspected yesterday that you were no mortal, but a visitor from the Nāt country, and now I am, of course, convinced of it."

The Nāt hung his head, and the judge proceeded, saying—

"Why have you come from your own world, taking upon yourself this form and shape, thereby causing so much pain and unhappiness to two innocent people?"

The Nāt, seeing that he could no longer carry on his course of deception, answered—

"In the season of the sun, and in that of the rain, for a greater time than I can count, I have lived in a tree in the forest, where this woodman comes every day. I troubled no one, and I was content till two days ago, when he felled my home to the ground with neither warning given to or permission asked of me. When other woodcutters have come, they have and do always crave permission of the Nāt residing in the tree to take from it even one branch. Therefore you must see that I have had just cause to be angry."

Manoo then said that the woodman had certainly been wrong in the way he had acted. Then, turning to the woman, he directed her and her husband to hang up a dried cocoa-nut on the best side of their hut for the Nāt to make his home in—an order which they promised to speedily obey.

The Nāt said that he was satisfied with that arrangement.

Then the three, thanking the judge, withdrew and went homewards.

From that time forth all Burmese people hung, and still hang, dried cocoa-nut in their houses for the spirits to dwell in.

A FABLE.

TWO dogs walked in the jungle together. The day was intensely hot, the rays of the sun, hardly tempered with any shade, fell through the towering bamboos and palm-trees down on their tired heads.

They had come far; the way was very rough, the undergrowth very tangled and dense. There seemed to be no end to it. Their vision in front was obscured by the extraordinary wealth of orchids and green foliage that was gracefully but thickly festooned from branch to branch.

Snakes glided away in the deep grass. Monkeys, squirrels, and birds of all kinds contended for the undisputed possession of the different trees.

"I am very tired; I don't think I can go much farther," said the lady dog, who was small and delicate, to her companion.

"So also am I," was the answer.

"It was foolish ever to have come," grumbled the first.

"It was your fault," snapped the second.

"I did not say it wasn't, did I?" retorted the other, who, female-like, had the last word.

Then they went on in silence for awhile. They both felt cross and hungry; and when you are hungry and a dog bananas are not very satisfying, and they were the only things near.

Presently they came to where a small stream flowed; the water was quite warm, but they drank it and were grateful.

Then they rested, going on again just when the last rays of the sun still showed above the dusky palm tops.

They hoped to reach a village before nightfall; but they were doomed to be disappointed. There was not a sign of any habitation near when the darkness began to close around. The stars twinkled brightly in a clear violet sky of wondrous brilliancy. Close beside them was a tiger's den—empty. They crept in and sank down, too weary to go further.

There were signs of its having been recently occupied, but they did not heed them; and gnawed ravenously at some half-eaten bones that were strewed about.

Then they curled themselves up in one corner and slept. After a few hours the lady dog woke up and looked about her. Through the opening she saw the moonlight falling on the country outside; everything was strangely still, save for the distant cry of the jackal, and the healthy snoring of her spouse, who reposed in the corner. She felt alarmed, she could not exactly have told why, and awakened her companion, who grumbled not a little at being thus rudely roused from his slumbers.

"Supposing," began his companion, not heeding his displeasure, "that the tiger was to return."

"What!" cried the listener, sharply jumping up in extreme alarm at the bare suggestion.

"Don't make that unearthly noise," said the lady, calmly. "I only said *supposing*, and I was going to ask you what we should do in such a case."

"Do! why, what could we do?—nothing, of course," was the somewhat contemptuous reply.

Just then an ominous crackling of the branches outside made them prick their ears. Creeping close to the opening, they looked out and saw in the distance a large tiger coming towards them, a white light, clear almost as the dawn, fell about him, showing his big head and striped back. The watchers trembled exceedingly, and their teeth rattled.

"There is no time to be lost," exclaimed the lady in a hoarse whisper. "We must trust to his never having seen any like us before, and we must try and frighten him."

"Humbug and nonsense! Fancy our frightening a tiger," said the gentleman dog with infinite scorn.

"Never mind, we'll try; you sit at the door while I remain in here. When I roar—well, you'll see the effect."

The dog very unwillingly took up his position at the entrance to the lair, and waited. In a second almost the great beast came slouching along; his gleaming eyes glanced hither and thither, and there was blood upon his mouth. Seeing the dog, he came to an abrupt pause, and stared, then came a little nearer, but very cautiously.

Just then there came a cry from within, accompanied by the words, "I am hungry, very hungry, and so are the little ones, they crave more tiger's flesh; be quick and bring it."

The tiger, hearing, waited for no more, but turned and fled into the night. He knew not what he had seen, but the words that he had heard had turned him cold with fear.

He flew on away into the wood, not heeding where he went. Then, just as the first rose flush of dawn overspread the sky, he sank down exhausted, with a cold perspiration all over him. He fell into a troubled, weary doze, from whence he was awakened by a banana dexterously aimed, hitting him in the eye. Looking up he saw a brown monkey swinging itself on the branch of a tree opposite, and regarding him with all that gleeful self-satisfaction which a monkey is alone capable of.

"Well, my friend," it cried, mockingly, "what has put you out? You look strangely pale and upset this morning."

"I have had sufficient cause," answered the tiger, rising and shaking himself; "for when I went home last night I found it filled by the most peculiar-looking animals that I have ever seen, who shouted for my flesh."

The listener cocked its ugly little head on one side as it munched bananas, and asked, "What were they like?"

"Don't ask me," exclaimed the tiger. "I was too frightened to see anything save that they were white."

The monkey flung itself up higher among the boughs and laughed loudly and long.

"If you don't stop that hideous noise I'll kill you," called out the tiger very angrily, regardless of the fact that he could not get within miles of his tormentor.

"Ha, ha! my friend," shouted the monkey, "the things that you were frightened of were two poor lean dogs, that went by here yesterday. What a great coward you are!"

"Coward or no coward, they would have killed me and eaten me."

"Eaten you! Oh, you great silly goose! With all your travels you don't know any more than that dogs can't kill you. You can kill dogs."

"I don't believe you," protested the tiger stolidly.

"Don't then," said the monkey, laconically, as he turned a somersault.

There was silence for a while. The tiger sat down dejectedly while the monkey watched him through the leaves and chuckled maliciously, continuing to eat noiselessly as he watched.

Having once had sufficient himself, he was not indisposed to be a little generous, so, taking some berries in one brown paw, he climbed down nearer the ground, and tendered them to his melancholy friend as an overture, saying as he did so—

"Eat and forget for awhile."

"I can never forget the loss of my dear home," was the melancholy reply.

"Nonsense," retorted the other one, who was practical, not sentimental, and who had a hundred homes all equally comfortable in the forest.

"It's no nonsense," said the tiger, shaking his head.

"Well," exclaimed the monkey, after a few seconds, "if you really are afraid to go back, which is ridiculous, I will come with you, for I fear no dogs."

"I wouldn't trust you," replied the tiger, ungraciously. "You have played me a scurvy trick or two before now."

The monkey became indignant, saying, "It is just like your mean, suspicious nature to speak so to a friend who, out of pure good nature, is willing to do you a turn. What motive can I have save generosity?—no good can accrue to me personally."

The tiger grunted an unwilling assent, and began to think seriously of accepting the offer.

"Well," he said at last, "if you will consent to be tied to my tail, and to go in first to the den, my back being to you, and face the dog, I am willing."

"Agreed," answered the monkey, who was an interfering little creature, and was longing to have his finger in the pie.

So they went, the monkey tied to his friend's tail, chattering all the way.

"Now," said the tiger, who was sullen and afraid as they came in sight of his lair, "if you don't behave fairly to me I will murder you, that's all."

"Never fear; I won't give you the opportunity of carrying out your amiable intention, because I shall act only as your true friend," replied the monkey.

Then he pushed aside the thick-growing foliage and entered into the cave, the tiger keeping as far away as possible, his hind-legs inside and the rest of him out. The dogs were lying down, but roused themselves on seeing their visitor.

"Well, monkey," shouted one, "so you have come at last, but that," looking behind him, "is a very lean tiger that you have brought. Why do you do so when you know that we like them so sleek and fat, and——" but the monkey heard no more. He was gone—jerked violently away by the tiger, who, suspecting his fidelity all along, was convinced of his perfidy by the words of the dog's greeting.

Away, away he sped, without turning back, over hill and dale, bump, bump, bang, bang, went the poor monkey's body, while he vainly protested his innocence in breathless, terrified shrieks. At last death came and ended his pain.

The two dogs sat and watched them till their eyes grew tired.

They laughed greatly as one said to the other, "See what happened to the monkey for interfering in other people's business."

THE STOLEN TREASURE.

IN a lonely part of a large forest there dwelt four wise men of India who owned a treasure consisting of gold, silver, and great jewels: like all property it was a source of great anxiety to its owners, for they always feared that it would be stolen from them. With that idea they constantly watched it, counted it, and changed its hiding-place; burying it sometimes under trees, or in a ruined well that stood not far distant; at other times with them in the house.

For many long years they had kept it safely thus, so safely indeed that gradually they grew a little less zealous in their guardianship: the confidence born of long and unmolested peace made them somewhat careless; and so in some inexplicable manner news of its existence floated to the ears of a young man who dwelt in the town not so many miles away, and he at once made up his mind that he would become possessed of it. Being wise he only took counsel of himself, and bided his time with much patience.

He made the acquaintance of the four recluses, and watched their movements and studied their habits with much diligence. He was a handsome, high-spirited youth, with manners that were frank and engaging, and the old men liked to see him and talk to him, soon growing to look forward to his visits.

Months passed, and he went to see them often. They conversed unreservedly before him and trusted him as one of themselves.

As time passed and no opportunity of taking the treasure offered itself, he began to be impatient, and was indeed almost reduced to despair when he learnt, to his inexpressible pleasure, that they intended going on a day's pilgrimage in the near future.

He laid his plans.

When the day came he rode to the forest on a pony, and, dismounting, fastened it near by as was his custom, and went within. The garden, with its moss-overgrown, decayed walls, was quite still save for the song of the birds. The sun fell through the leaves of the trees and made brilliant patches of light on the grass.

The rooms of the house were dark and cool and empty. There were the broken remains of a meal and various things belonging to the absent masters scattered about. The visitor looked round and about him carefully, peering here and there, then, having quite satisfied himself that only he and the feathered world shared the stillness, he smiled.

Some hours later the pilgrims returned home: they had been far and were wearied; they rested for awhile, then ate their evening meal and prepared to make ready for the night. As was customary with them they went to look at the treasure where they had put it in an upper room, to find to their unspeakable horror and dismay that it was gone. They looked on one another in mute amazement and despair; they beat their breast; there were no words to describe what they felt in that hour when they bewailed its loss in a helpless, hopeless way.

After awhile one of them said—

"He who has come here so many times of late with fair words and fairer smiles, it is he who hath done this thing."

The others agreed that it was only he who could have, for no one else had ever penetrated to their abode or shared their confidence. Too late they bitterly rued having ever received the stranger.

They sat long that night talking. One said—

"We have no proof save our own conviction that he whom we met as a friend and a brother has robbed us; therefore what can we do?"

The others answered him—

"We will seek the King, to our requests he has always leant a kind and willing ear."

Meanwhile homeward through the sultry night rode a horseman with a heavy load.

When the dawn broke, they who had been robbed set out together to seek the Court of the King.

His Majesty, who was revered for his goodness, had one daughter who to a keen intellect united great beauty, and was renowned throughout her father's dominions and even in countries beyond the sea.

Whenever the King or his ministers were perplexed as to how to act in any particular matter they invariably consulted the Princess, who on each and all such occasions had guided them aright; while no chicanery or fraud ever passed her undetected.

All that was brave, lofty, and good she admired, honoured, and followed. All that was mean, low, and dishonest she abhorred.

United to a powerful mind were many womanly, gracious, and charitable qualities, which made her beloved in humble circles as well as respected in high ones.

Therefore when the four petitioners sought the King, it was with the idea of humbly pleading for the Princess's assistance.

The King, who knew them, received them at once on their arrival and listened to all that they had to say, agreeing with them in their suspicions. He asked them, when he had heard their story, if they could identify the property if they were to see it anywhere; to which they answered, "Yes."

Then, bidding them rest and refresh themselves, he went himself to the apartments of his daughter and told her the tale that he had heard. She was very much interested, and gladly promised to do what she could, telling her father that if the young man could be found and brought to the palace she fancied that she could restore to them their lost goods.

Whereupon the King consulted the four, and a messenger was sent to search and bring the young fellow with as little delay as possible. The envoy of His Majesty found him whom they desired with but little difficulty, who received the royal summons with much astonishment and some fear. Instinctively he felt that it was with regard to the stolen jewels that he was sent for, and he trembled not a little as he set out.

Were the theft ever to be discovered he knew full well that his punishment would not be a light one. Almost he felt inclined to regret that he had ever embarked on so hazardous a course, but then the memory of the shining heaps of gold and silver and the glittering stones, and all that they represented, came to him, and he laughed and shook off all feelings of fear; for how, after all, he said to himself, could they prove that it was he who was the thief?

When he arrived at the palace, therefore, he was quite light-hearted, and walked through the lines of servants with a haughty, self-confident air.

They ushered him through many halls and at last into a large and most beautifully decorated apartment situated at the end of a long vista of salons. The four walls had bas-reliefs of graceful figures of women in coloured marble and uncut jewels. The hangings were of ivory satin, embroidered with elephants and dragons in dead gold. From the ceiling were suspended magnificent lamps of many finely blended colours. A large fountain splashed softly near by; the floor was strewn with tiger skins; the air was heavy with strong perfume; while the light from without stole in subdued and cool through green blinds. But what riveted the visitor's attention beyond all else was a couch of immense dimensions stretching across the upper end of the room, reclining on which amongst many cushions was a woman; overhead was a canopy of fringed cloth supported by delicately chased silver poles inlaid with turquoises. On a table of mother-of-pearl stood some cheroots and a glass globe of water. Several attendants, gorgeously attired, lounged near, and created a breeze with fans made of real roses.

The lady herself was very handsome, with a clear skin of an almost olive colour, great eyes of a velvety darkness, and a soft, slow, sweet smile; pearls clasped her throat, diamonds shone on her fingers, while gold bracelets glittered on her slender bare ankles. She motioned her somewhat bewildered visitor to seat himself near, and signed to the attendants to withdraw.

He felt terribly nervous in the presence of this royal lady: she watched him in silence for a few moments, fanning herself languidly the while; she was uncertain as to how to open the conversation. He was very handsome, certainly, she thought, as she looked, and with a figure as lithe and graceful as that of a panther.

She raised herself a little and leant forward slightly; he started and looked at her apprehensively.

"I suppose," she began, "that you are wondering why I sent for you?"

The tones of her voice were strangely liquid and clear.

The young man murmured something indistinctly in response.

She continued, "But for some time past, when the King and myself have gone abroad, we have seen you often and have desired to know you."

The listener was trembling so with joy, relief, and surprise at hearing such words, that he could find naught to say in reply.

Then she, perceiving his agitation, spoke to him gently and kindly for a few minutes, in order to give him time to recover his self-possession. Then, when he was more composed, she asked him many questions about himself—questions which he gladly answered. Then after a while she bade him go and to return on the morrow.

So he went from the seductive presence of the Princess with his head in a whirl, and feeling as if he dwelt no longer on earth but in Nirvana.

On the morrow he returned, and for many days following, not a question was ever asked. He was ushered always into the same room, where he was greeted most graciously.

On the occasion of his fourth visit, after the Princess had conversed with him on many subjects, she asked him somewhat suddenly if he was betrothed or married.

And when he answered that he was not it seemed to him that she appeared pleased. Then a long silence fell between them, which he of course did not attempt to break.

"My friend," she said at last, and her manner was somewhat nervous and embarrassed, "I am glad that your affections are not placed elsewhere, because I myself, strange as it is for a woman to tell a man, desire to wed with you. To my father's Court have come many who have sought my hand in marriage, but in none have I seen those qualities which I admire and esteem——" she paused.

The low, thrilling words stole on the listener's ear in sweet, subdued cadence. Did he hear aright? He doubted it; he feared that he only dreamt.

Then he looked at her where she sat, with her shimmering jewels glancing a thousand hues, and his heart throbbed and his brain reeled, and he was as if drunk with wine.

He knew not how to answer this beautiful, gracious lady.

How she must love him, he thought, when she could so stoop from her high estate. He dropped on his knees before her. "Ah," he murmured, "where could I find fitting expressions in which to tell you what I feel? Your words have lifted me to complete Nirvana, I shall never dwell on earth again. Speech is but a poor thing often, therefore I will not say much. Deeds are best; it is by them, O Princess, that you shall read my heart."

She smiled, and her eyes were softly tender as they met his.

"There is but one thing," she said, after a few moments; "my father must not be told till after we are married; he would not sanction our union, though he will forgive us afterwards. Therefore you must take me hence, away from out the kingdom for some time; then, when my father's just anger shall have faded, as it surely will, we will return together."

The young man listened in rapt attention, scarcely crediting even yet his own great fortune.

"And yet I scarcely see," gravely pursued the Princess, after a short silence, "how it can be managed."

She rose as she spoke and advanced to where a box of ivory, inlaid with opals, stood, touched a spring and opened it.

"See," she cried, "this is all the money I own," taking in her hands a few small worthless pieces of silver; "I have never required money till now, all that I have ever wanted has been always beside me."

"Do not fear if it is only money that you need," answered the young man; "for of that I have more than enough."

"Ah! is that so?" she exclaimed eagerly, turning to him a face of glad surprise.

"At home," he continued, "I have much of jewels and gold which I got but a little while back; sufficient to keep us in that luxury which is due to your rank, for many a year to come."

"Go and fetch it," urged the Princess, "and return here at nightfall, and I will go with thee to another life—a life of happiness such as this world seldom holds."

Her great eyes glittered as she spoke.

He read in her words, her looks, and her gestures only the fond impatience of a love long, secret, and denied.

He prostrated himself, and saying, "I will return at nightfall," left her to hurry on his errand.

In the early evening, when the darkness had only just fallen, he drove in a carriage to the palace; he left it at a little distance from the great gold entrance, and taking on his person much of his stolen treasure, he was ushered into the Princess's room; the swinging lamps were lit and shed a faint radiance on all around.

She was by herself, and greeted him in a manner that left nothing to be desired.

Wishing to assure her of the existence of that money and those jewels that he had spoken of, and feeling nervously elated, he drew from the recesses of his turban and sash a handful of great stones, that were as rivers of light; she gave a woman's delighted cry as she took them in her hands.

He smiled, well pleased, and tendered a great ruby of wondrous size and blood-red fire.

"These are but a few of what I have," he said.

"How rich you must be!" she exclaimed, "From whence did all these things come?"

"Ah, Princess, what matter whence they came? Sufficient it is that now they are yours."

As he spoke she, unseen by him, touched a gong of curious workmanship that stood near.

Then she held the stones up to the light, praising their beauty and worth, and asking many questions.

A short while passed and then a great door at the end of the room opened and the King entered, followed by the four fakirs, and advanced to where his daughter sat.

The young man's heart beat in alarm at the sight of those whom he had robbed. And the Princess's first words did not tend to decrease the feeling.

"Are these some of the treasures that you have lost?" she asked, handing to the elder of the four the biggest of the diamonds and the rubies. He took them in his hand, then passed them to the others, saying, at the same time—

"These are ours."

"There stands the thief, then," said the Princess, pointing to the now cowering shaking figure of the culprit, who looked piteously from one to the other, feeling at the same time very enraged with himself for having been so easily caught in the trap that had been laid for him. "It is for you," continued the

Princess, addressing herself to the four, "when your entire treasure has been restored to you, to name his punishment."

The elder of them answered—

"We are so rejoiced to regain that which we had feared was lost for ever, Princess, that we are willing that he should go forth unchastised; his conscience, and what it will say to him, will be his punishment."

"That would be too light a sentence; for I doubt much if he has any conscience," said the lady, as she seated herself.

"Then, Princess, will you relieve us by sentencing him yourself, as you best will?" craved the four.

"No," she answered, "that I cannot do, I might be too harsh—I have convicted him; let His Majesty, who is ever lenient, name his punishment."

Then they all turned to the King, who said—

"I command that he be banished from this land for ever, and any property that he has, or is likely to have, be confiscated."

THE VIGIL OF MAH MAY.

MAH MAY was a little Burmese girl who kept a small stall filled with cheroots in one of the crowded many-coloured streets of Rangoon. There she sat all through the sultry, languorous days smoking and waiting, with philosophical calm, for customers; now and then a great, big, well-fed looking Indian would stop and handle her goods, and, grumbling perhaps a little, would eventually buy; or a lean Chinaman, in baggy blue trousers, would pause and smile and talk awhile; or some little naked child would come and beg one for nothing; or the black coolies, their silver belts glittering in the sunlight, would cluster round and bargain and quarrel among themselves, perhaps, in the end, throwing her goods back to her with no very complimentary language; or a "Chetty,"[1] airily attired in scanty white muslin, his shaved head protected by a big cotton umbrella, would come and haggle over the annas as a poor Burman would never dream of doing; then, again, a well-to-do woman of her own race, dressed in silk, and with gold bracelets on her wrists, would purchase, but they were always, as Mah May used to say with a shake of her small head, the meanest of all.

She was a bright little girl, though very poor; often hungry, and always wretchedly clad.

For two years past she had squatted behind her tray, in the hot, hard, cruel glare, when the sun beat on the flat-roofed white

---

[1] Indian money-lender

houses mercilessly; when even the river, with its forests of ships, seemed to cease to flow; when all things were gasping and weary and the gharry wallahs slept soundly, and the poor lean ponies tried to flick the flies off their backs with their tails; when the Indian shopkeepers stretched themselves on wooden beds just in the shadow of their door-ways and snored away, dreaming of rupees and curry; while only the pariah dogs scratched and smelt in the road for something to eat. No one stirred; the drowsy influence of the heat seemed universal. Or on the dull wet days, when the sky was clouded and rain poured down, soaking everything through and through, and the thin coloured dresses clung pitifully round their owners' dark forms, and nobody had time to think of buying as they passed on in the warm, damp, oppressive atmosphere. Still Mah May sat, no matter what the season, rolling her cheroots, cutting betel chews, and crooning some little song to herself. At mid-day she ate some rice, and got a draught of water from a pump not far distant. Often some one was kind, and gave her some fruit or a cake; oftener they were unkind, but oftener still they were indifferent.

It was a hard life—very, and she was only seventeen. Yet was she content. Nature had been her nurse. The sun and the rain had made her what she was—a hardy, honest, upright little soul, envying and hating no one.

When the shadows grew long and the green shutters of the shops closed, Mah May rolled up her wares and wended her way homewards through the noisy, many-hued crowds to a miserable wooden hut, which stood in dirty yellow water, spanned by a rotten plank, and was situated in one of the poorest and most squalid quarters of the town—a quarter in which poverty, in its most hideous form, stalked. Half-clothed men, women and children of all ages, dwelt together there, and kept life in them as best they could.

In the huts there was scarce one piece of furniture, save perhaps a bed or a roll of matting or a ragged purdah.

The scorpions, the white ants, and the great toads held high revel. Amidst rows, hard words, evil things, cries of little children, and growls of half-starved dogs Mah May dwelt, and was happy.

She did not know of any better life than hers. The day passed in the fresh air under the changeless azure of the skies and the night curled up in a corner of the hut, with the purple stars looking down through some chink in the roof; and knowing of any other, it is doubtful if she would have cared to exchange.

Mah Khine, a black-browed woman whom Mah May had lived with as long as she could remember, was very good and kind to her in her own way; but she had many children tugging at her skirt, and her life was a very hard one. She was married to an Indian who had nearly all the faults of his by no means faultless race; his past had been bad, his present was even more so.

He counted the cost of anything, done or undone, as small if it only brought in pice; pice sufficient to procure "toddy,"[2] the hot, horrible, poisonous stuff kept in the little shop by a Chinaman in one of the narrow, tortuous bye-lanes of the native quarter. To him it mattered nothing that his children had oftentimes not enough to eat, and that the lines about his wife's patient mouth deepened.

The passion for drink possessed him, to the exclusion of all other feelings.

Stretched on a wooden settle in the crowded, dirty shop that abutted on the still dirtier street, reeking with filth and smells, he passed his time sunk in a semi-conscious stupor.

---

2 "Toddy" is composed of the juice of palms, and sold in those shops when fermented.

The proprietor looked upon Moulla Khan as one of the best customers he had.

For him was his smile the sweetest, to him was he most accommodating in the matter of money.

Of a day the frequenters of the place were comparatively few, but when the night crept on, Pun Lun lit up his place with many sickly oil lamps, whose light showed up the gaudy signboard with its ill-written "Toddy Shop" on it, surrounded by a curious design in Chinese, and drew the human moths round in dozens to smoke, drink, play, and talk. Indian, Burmese, all countries were represented there in that crowded, noisy, dirty place. The babel of many tongues broke on the ear afar off.

The neighbourhood was a notoriously bad one, so that the fighting and sickening sound of blows that usually ended these gatherings of convivial spirits excited no comment.

Even the deep groans from those who, wounded, lay helplessly for many hours gained no sympathy or succour of any kind.

Often, but in vain, in the hot, sulphurous nights Mah Khine had found her way there, and begged of the great coarse brute whom she called husband to return with her, but for a long time past she had ceased to plead, realising how useless it was.

And yet, strangely, with all his drunkenness and cruelty, the faithful soul refused to desert or even see him as he really was. He had been the chosen one of her girlhood, when she, young and pretty, had left her people to wed this stranger out of India.

They had deemed her disgraced by the union.

They had been well-to-do people, and would have married her to one of her own race.

Her life had held many bitter, unhappy years, but she was proud in her way, and from her lips no word or moan had ever passed.

Children had come and multiplied, and though the wants of such people are very few, often they had not the wherewithal to supply them.

But of late years things had been better, for Mah Khine, who had a keen eye for business, had made and saved a little unknown to every one except Mah May.

The money was kept buried away in a teak-wood box in a corner of their damp, worm-eaten house.

Mah Khine's cherished ambition, trader that she was, was to open a little shop, as many of her class did.

A little place filled with miscellaneous articles: pillows, lacquer boxes, wooden trays, crockery, pewter pans, some sandals, and perhaps, there was no knowing—that is, if she was lucky—some tameins and silk potsos for the men.

There behind it the proud possessor, she dreamt that she would sit and roll the cheroots and have her children by her, keeping an eye on the younger as they played.

This picture Mah Khine often painted to herself; it was her ideal of earthly bliss. She dreamt of it by day and night, but kept it locked up in her own heart.

Anything that she could spare from what she made by washing the clothes of her richer neighbours she put by so carefully, handling it so fondly, storing it so cautiously: grimy brown pice, little silver pieces, one or two soiled, crumpled notes, how often she looked at them and counted them and took them in her lean brown hands! She would start out of her sleep, fearing some one had stolen her treasure, that represented the scraping together of two hard, long years.

There was some little history attached to every coin.

She remembered how each one was gained, every circumstance of toil or sacrifice through which it was put by.

And not a soul knew, not a soul save Mah May and herself; Mah May she could trust. Mah May loved her, and was as honest and true as a little dog.

Mah Khine never left the box in the house with no one to mind it, for fear it should be taken, though for two years gone by it had rested securely and undisturbed in its hiding-place.

The knowledge of its existence, and what in the end it was to accomplish, leant a courage to her to bear with the blows, the sickness, and the abject poverty of her surroundings; it upheld her, it leant a brightness to her eyes, a lightness to her feet when they would have been otherwise pitifully weary. When she spoke there was oftentimes a strange ring of gladness in her voice; for Hope, that wonderful strengthener, dwelt with her.

So time went on, and it wanted but three months for the money to be complete. They had been rarely lucky.

Mah May had sold well every day. Mah Khine had had much to do. A great content abode with her. Even the morose, savage manner of her husband troubled her but little.

The children flew at his approach, and hid behind the mud hill close by, or their mother's ragged skirts, or anywhere they could, and she soothed and comforted the little trembling ones as she best could, and on her face was a happy smile.

"At last! at last!" she thought.

One warm, clear night, when the sky glittered with stars, and a young moon showed against it, Mah Khine made ready to take some silks that she had been washing home. She had promised them, for it was the eve of a great Buddhist feast. It was a long way for her to go, right across the town, but she did not mind. So she cleared up the remains of their evening rice, swept the floor with her straw besom, filled the water-chatty standing in the corner afresh, bade Mah May to watch carefully; and Mah

May assured her, as she had often done before, that if any one was ever to find out their secret, the money they should never have, save they killed her first. So Mah Khine took up her bundle and went forth into the radiance of the night.

Mah May looked after her until she was out of sight, and then squatted down, smoking.

The hours went by; the lights were put out in the huts. Mah May felt very sleepy and tired where she sat, but she was good—she remained awake, staring out into space....

A tall, dark figure stood before her. It was Moulla Khan; he had not been home for two days. His eyes were blood-shot, his turban disarranged. He stood over her, and looked down at her. She trembled a little; she feared him greatly. She stirred uneasily, but nevertheless met his look without flinching.

He only uttered one word, and that in a voice which drink had rendered hoarse and thick.

"Money." He spoke in Hindustani.

"I have none," she answered him in the same tongue.

He gave a sort of gurgling laugh.

"Look you," he muttered, "I know there is money hidden somewhere—pice and annas and rupees—and I will have it; I know it, I tell you, I know it."

"There is none," the girl replied. She had risen; she had her back to the hole in the wall where the money was.

"Give it to me," he cried, in a voice of frantic rage.

"I do not know who has told you this thing," she said, "but it is not true."

She felt chilly with fright. She knew that, once his suspicion aroused, he would search till he found. She would be powerless to protect it. Tears dimmed the fond eyes of the child. She knew, none better, all the toil, privations, and hopes that lay in that poor little box.

Yet what could she do? She was so small and her strength so puny. If he searched he would find it; its hiding-place was not so secure as to be proof against those cruel fingers.

Though all Mah Khine's future lay there, she gave no sign of fear. She kept her ground boldly. He shook her savagely, when she stood. She was wondering who could have told him. She watched him with a dull, throbbing brain move unsteadily round the wretched room, groping by the light of the moon; feeling, feeling everywhere along the wall for holes; turning over all the things; then, with a muttered word or two, out he went on to the rafters, made of mud, behind, into a little piece of ground; but there was nothing, nothing anywhere. Her breath came a little quicker, a little more freely. Perhaps, after all—but, with a bound, he was by her side. He nearly wrenched her slender, childish wrists off. "It is there!" he cried in triumph.

She set her strong white teeth in his black arm; but with a brutal gesture he flung her light weight from him. She fell with a dull, heavy thud. He did not heed her for awhile, searching eagerly, thirstily, his eyes glittering with cruel greed.

At last he drew it forth triumphantly, the poor little shabby treasure-house, and took the money, letting some drop in his haste, hiding it with trembling, feverish hands in his white linen jacket.

Then he put the box back, and turned to Mah May. He looked; she was very still; he crept nearer and nearer, and his cowardly soul shrank within him. The moonbeams had found her out and fell upon her thin, upturned face. He peered round, he held his very breath; no one was stirring, there was silence everywhere. His dark, acquiline face was as cunning as that of any fox cub.

He paused for a second or two. Then, as if a sudden thought struck him, he gathered her up hastily in his arms.

She was a little heavy, but he was strong.

The river, that was drifting outward to the ocean, and the moon were the only things that shared the secret of that night with him.

And they guard their secrets well.

"If Mah May wanted the money, I would have given it to her, for I loved her; she need not have left me," Mah Khine said, with a great sorrow and sense of desolate despair in her heart, and tears in her honest eyes, when Moulla Khan told his tale.

She never learnt different—she never will—unless, indeed, the day dawns when the sea shall give up its dead.

THE PETITION TO THE KING.

IN the reign of King Mindoon, who was the father of King Theebaw, a servant sent a petition to him in which he set forth that he had been his humble and faithful servitor before his accession to the throne, but now, although seven long years had gone by since then, he had remained forgotten and unnoticed. Continuing in this strain for a space, he ended with the following parable:—

In the Zita country there lived a King who had a son named Padoma, whom he sent to Thakada to be educated, and with him he sent a young attendant called Thomana.

For three years they stayed at Thakada, at the end of which period the Prince, having completed his studies, prepared to return home; on their way, travelling by easy stages, they paused at a small village situated in deep-wooded lands, where a great feast was being held. Hundreds of people had gathered there from all parts. A large tent was erected in one part, where a banquet was spread, to partake of which they humbly begged the Prince.

And he willingly accepted.

On the ground had been spread matting, on a part of which a gorgeously embroidered scarlet cloth with a golden fringe was put for the Prince, and a white one, less magnificently worked and with a silver fringe, for his friend and attendant Thomana.

When they had seated themselves, the rest of the company did likewise, remaining, however, at a distance, and separated by a cord.

Now Thomana was very learned in astrology, having read and thought deeply on that subject, and he knew as soon as he saw the Prince seat himself on the red cloth that he would become King upon that very day.

It was a brilliant assembly, every one clad in delicate silks of all hues, and glittering with jewels. The feast lasted long, it seemed, indeed, as if the constant succession of dishes was to be an endless one. All were in the best of spirits, and laughed and talked greatly.

When the Prince had finished his repast, he was shown into an inner tent, where a couch of the same royal colour had been placed, and in front was a slightly raised platform of bamboo, draped with violet and rose-pink satin, richly worked and lighted with lamps, that shed a subdued radiance round and about the little graceful figures of several dancing girls who had been bidden to dance for his royal highness.

Their dresses were so formed as to represent armour, and on their heads were similar coverings. They performed peculiar, dreamy, kind of movements, amidst a mist of varying hues. The Prince was much interested, and postponed retiring until late.

Thomana, having bidden his royal master good-night, felt disinclined for sleep, so, strolling into a park-like demesne that was adjacent, he seated himself under a large tree, whose branches spread for a considerable way, and became lost in thought.

It was a glorious night, with not a sound in the air save the soft whirr of some purpled-eyed or golden-winged insect as it floated by in the darkness. As he sat there musing on the events of the evening and the future of the Prince, two large leaves fell from above into his hand: one was old and withered, the other was fresh and green. "Ah," he murmured, as he looked at them, "in the same way as an old and a young leaf drops from the tree, so may a man full of years and one who is in the morning of life die at the same time."

In the midst of his meditations, which lasted long, he became a rahan,[3] and was taken from the garden to the Gandremadana Mountains. At the same time a chariot of pearl, drawn by four pure white horses with trappings of gold, was on its way to the Prince to carry him back, as his father had died that day. Following the chariot came four ministers and a train of Court officials, accompanied by soldiers.

They awakened the sleeping Prince and acquainted him with their news. Then, when he was prepared, he stepped into the chariot that was waiting, and was borne with all speed to the palace, where he was proclaimed King the following day with the utmost pomp, ceremony, and rejoicings.

In his new life, and amidst his many duties and responsibilities, he entirely forgot the existence of his attendant, who had been his constant companion for three years; therefore his absence passed unrecorded and unnoticed; for what the King forgets the courtiers must never be unwise enough to remember.

At the end of thirty years, when the King was getting old, he remembered Thomana, and wondered greatly where he might be. Whereupon he immediately caused it to be made known throughout his dominions that he would give a lac of rupees to any one who should give him any news of his lost servant.

Now Thomana, owing to his great piety and powers of clairvoyance, became aware immediately of the fact that his old master had recollected him, and desired his presence. Therefore he went at once to the garden where he had been seated before he attained his rahanship so many years before.

---

3 "Rahan," *i.e.*, one possessed of supernatural powers.

Close by the tree, under whose branches he had sat, were four shepherd boys, their flocks grazing near, while they themselves talked together of the big reward that the King had offered for news of his old servant.

Thomana, coming through the leafy aisles, heard them, and accosted them, declaring that he was the person whom the King desired. They rose and glanced at him doubtingly.

"Let two of you," he said, "go to the palace and tell His Majesty, that I await him here." To which they assented.

A short while passed, and then an immense carriage, glittering like gold and silver in the sun, and followed by others less imposing, could be seen coming rapidly along the white winding road. Pulling up at the entrance, the King himself alighted, and came through the gates, that were all brazen and blazoned, straight towards Thomana, his arms outstretched to embrace him; but he whom he would have greeted so cordially stopped him, saying—

"I am now a rahan; with men, their feelings, their passions, their brief triumphs, and sorrows, likes and dislikes, I have no affinity." Then he folded his arms and stood in silence.

His face was very cold and still.

The King, looking at him, saw that he was poorly clad, and bent, and thin, and pressed him to return to the Court, where he promised him money and many wives.

But the rahan answered—

"I do not need wealth, nor any of the poor fleeting pleasures that this world can offer. Let your Majesty come with me instead, and visit my abode of rest."

"What is it like, this place," inquired the King in wonder, "that it can render its inhabitants indifferent to what we esteem the most desirable of all things in this life?"

"It is situated far from here," replied Thomana, "and the approach to it is a broad, long avenue of gorgeous blossoms, such as you have never dreamed of, that bloom for ever, with a perfume that is at once dreamy, drowsy, and infinitely sweet; vast sprays of water spring from the mouths of silver dragons; over head the branches of trees interlace, showing but a strip of blue sky through their quivering leaves. For hours can you wander amongst these mazes of roses, this wonder of colour and beauty. At the end of the grove is situated an immense tree, larger than aught that you have seen and higher than any eye could reach. It is surrounded by columns of marble that glow like jewels. Here the nāts and fairies dwell, with nothing to disturb their seclusion and solitude save the sound of falling waters and the song of birds. While over all is cast such a spell as this life does not hold. Ah! beside the perfection of that world, how poor and valueless are the things of this! There one talks with the gods and dwells in worlds beyond the sun. There is no room for regrets or for desires. There every one is beautiful, therefore we do not covet beauty. There wealth is common to all, therefore we do not desire it. There all are equal, and love and goodness are the aim and end of all things. Come and see for yourself," he added.

And the King, marvelling greatly at what he had heard, went. And there, in the midst of those divine surroundings, with naught to disturb the mind from the good, he wandered, awed and silent, but not afraid. In those cool, wide halls of bliss, all memories of grosser things and ways faded into nothingness. He forgot his kingdom, and was by it forgot.

THE PRIEST'S PETITION.

IT was the custom for the heir to the throne of the kingdom of Ava to be placed, while young, in a monastery with the priests, to be instructed in a manner suitable to the position that he was destined to occupy. Prince Min Goung, while a boy, was put under the special care of the Phoongyee Shin Ah Tah Thaya—a prudent and learned man, who gave all his time and wisdom to his pupil.

Min Goung was of a proud and wilful nature, and one who would not willingly bend his haughty head to any yoke, however light and silken.

One day his reverend teacher punished him, for persistent bad writing, somewhat severely—an act which he regretted afterwards, thinking, perhaps, that he had been over harsh.

Time passed away. The King died, and the young Prince was crowned. Then the priest began to fear that his former pupil might do him some harm, for he imagined that he had never forgiven him the liberty he had taken in chastising him. So he quitted his retreat, and fled to Prome for safety. Disliking his enforced banishment, he determined to write and crave for pardon; and in the course of his long appeal, written on palm leaves, was the following story:—

"There was a king of Bayanathee, learned and merciful, who had a hundred sons, each of whom, when old enough, was given into the hands of a carefully selected instructor to be taught those subjects for which he had the greatest taste. When each was grown up and had completed his education, he was appointed a governor of a portion of the royal dominions; and so ninety-nine of the Princes had been educated and been presented to the King and received their appointments. Prince Thanwara was the youngest of them, and was taken care of by a distinguished minister, who began and continued his instruction in a way that was very suitable to the quick natural intelligence of the boy; and when the time came for Thanwara to go to his father, his teacher accompanied him.

"When they came before the King—who was seated on a throne of silver and agate, with golden doors behind him—he asked his son if he had learnt and completed the same course of studies as his elder brothers, and the young Prince answered him —

"'I am sufficiently qualified, sire, to take upon me the same duties and responsibilities as those of my brothers who have gone before.'

"The King was satisfied with the reply; and then, after a while, the Prince and his tutor returned to their home.

"Talking to the tutor before he slept, Thanwara said—

"'If the King my father offers me the same position as he has bestowed on my brothers, will it be well with me to accept it?'

"The teacher made answer thus—

"'If a man, O Prince, desires to partake of the Bandaya fruit, which only grows in Nirvana, can he obtain it from its tree from the distance of a hundred yujanas (eight hundred miles), or would he rather not stand under the tree and take the fruit with a hooked bamboo? In the same way, if you wish to sit on the throne it is best for you not to go from here, but to remain in the shadow of the palace.'

"The prince listened, and then, when he had heard to the end, he said—

"'Then, my teacher, when to-morrow I go before my father, and he asks me my desires, what shall I make reply?'

"'Ask of him to bestow on you the rents of the bazaars and the produce or the royal gardens within the city gates.'

"'Of what benefit would such be to me?'

"'The greatest benefit, my son. For those who have money have power, of which truth I will give you an illustration:—

"'A timid doe in the forest, when it once sees a leopard, will fly, and hiding carefully, will not venture to stir out again for many days and nights; but on the other hand, retiring as it is by nature, it will, if a person constantly feed it, so far lose its timidity as to approach him and take from his hand. Therefore, my son, if you give presents often to the favourites and the advisers of the King, you will gain their confidence and their liking.'

"On the following day, when the Prince reached the palace, and his father asked him to name the province that he wished to govern, he answered thus:—

"'My brothers have all gone from you to distant parts of the world to guard over your vast possessions; let me then remain here to be your Majesty's attendant, and render you that care and assistance in sickness, in health, and in trouble, or any other trial, that affection can alone offer.'

"The old King was pleased, and granted unhesitatingly what he was asked.

"From that day forth Thanwara received the rents and profits of the bazaars and gardens, and took up his residence near the throne, in the white palace of his father.

"Gradually his winning manners, his deference to his elders, his many thoughtful and beautiful gifts, and, lastly, his own piety and learning, gained for him the first place in the hearts of those who were about the Court.

"So the years fled away, and were counted with the past.

"But when the tenth year was young, the King's health failed him; he felt that the sands of his life were nearly run. So about him he gathered his ministers and advisers. After they had expressed their sympathy and regret at finding him ill, they inquired which of all his sons he would best like to wear his crown when he was gone.

"The dying King raised himself from the low couch on which he was reclining, and, propped by many cushions, answered their question in this wise:

"'A hermit was one day coming from his lonely Himalayan abode through a forest. Over his head, as a sunshade, he had an enormous flower, called the kakayu mala, which is found, as you are aware, only in the Nāt Country, and its fragrance reached to the distance of one yujana (eight miles). On his way he encountered four fairies, each of whom saw and coveted the blossom. They all in turn asked him for it, but he said, in reply to their request, "I can only give it to the most virtuous and the most excellent of you all."

"'Whereupon each protested, all contending for the honour.

"'But the hermit, who was discreet and prudent, said, "How can I, who have no means to judge, decide? To me you all seem worthy of it, equally charming, and deserving in all respects, therefore had I four flowers I would divide them gladly between you; but as there is but one, and that one incapable of division, we will refer the matter to the King of the Nāt Country, who has the all-discerning eye."

"'So they went.

"'They had not to travel far before they came to his green and gracious kingdom.

"'They made straight for the beautiful ivory palace where the King dwelt, and were ushered into where he sat on his throne, composed entirely of the very flowers.

"'He inquired what brought them before him.

"'They told him. Then he thought for a little time, while they waited at a distance. When he called them to him and said—

"'"There is a rahan residing in the Kisokok Mountains to whom I will present a golden pineapple; then the four of you shall go and seek him and ask him for it. The person whom he shall give the golden apple to, that person shall be the most worthy in every way to be the recipient of the flower."

"'They thanked him, withdrew, and started for the Kisokok Mountains.

"'When they arrived there the rahan requested each fairy to take up her position according to the four directions of the earth—north, south, east and west—which they did, while each clamoured for the prize.

"'Then the rahan asked them their names, to which the eldest replied, "Thada" ("Charity"); the second, "Thati" ("Peace"); the third, "Hiri" ("Modesty"); the fourth, "Ootoppa" ("Virtue").

"'When the rahan heard he gave the golden apple into the hands of Ootoppa, saying, as her name represented, she was the most deserving. Then she went to the hermit, who presented her with the beautiful flower, and from that moment she was esteemed the most virtuous and most excellent of all women in the Nāt Country.

"'Therefore,' continued the old King, addressing the ministers around him, 'you must be the hermit in this case.'

"Before that day was over he was dead, and was interred with great honours and many lamentations.

"Then the advisers, with no delay and no hesitation, elected Prince Thanwara to succeed his father; but when the news reached the other sons in their distant territories they were filled with wrath. The second sent to his elder brother a letter, in which he said that the ministers of their late father were weak and corrupt, and very wanting in foresight in allowing themselves to be persuaded into placing the youngest of all on the throne, thereby disregarding the principle of the ancient rule of succession; for (continued he) in the Ahrottaya Country there was a King who had three children, two sons and a daughter, born of the chief Queen. When the eldest son was sixteen years of age the Queen died. The second Queen thereupon became chief, by whom the King had a son, and when that son reached eight years of age the King was bitten by a snake, a fact which frightened him greatly. The Queen, however, who was quick to think and very brave, sucked the poison from the bite. The King, being filled with gratitude, asked her to make any request that she liked, which he would grant, whereupon she immediately begged that her son might be selected as the heir to the throne, and to her inexpressible satisfaction the King gave his consent.

"A while later his Majesty sent for Narada, a soothsayer, who was asked to calculate his term of life. Narada told him that he would live twelve more years. The King then sent for his three children by the dead queen and acquainted them with the soothsayer's prophecy, telling them at the same time that they must quit the Court and find a home elsewhere for twelve years.

"Sorrowing greatly, they obeyed. After nine years the King died of grief for the absence of the children that he had sent from him.

"The Queen lost no time in scheming to put the crown upon her son's head. But the chief minister opposed her, saying that the eldest boy still lived and could not be put aside.

"Then he took the crown and all the insignia of royalty, and with many attendants and great state travelled to where the eldest son resided, and offered the throne to him.

"The Prince met him with the argument that the King's commands extended to twelve years, and that, as only nine had elapsed, his step-brother must reign for three years. Then he gave the minister a pair of slippers, worked with wheat, to give to his half-brother, with the direction that they were to be placed on the judgment-seat, declaring, as he did so, that if any decision is illegal or contrary to the right, the slippers would of themselves rise and touch each other as a protest.

"'Wherefore,' continued the brother's epistle, 'as the ministers have not paid you the respect of deferring to you in the matter, we should prepare to go to war with Thanwara.' The elder brother, on receiving the above, addressed a letter to his youngest brother, in which he requested him to surrender the crown or to prepare for hostilities.

"Prince Thanwara sought the advice of his chief minister in his perplexity, and he told him that, according to religion, he must not oppose his elder brother.

"'Then,' asked Thanwara, 'what am I to do?'

"The chief minister answered: 'Divide all the property in the kingdom into one hundred shares, and give each equally.'

"And it was accordingly done, upon which the eldest brother, being quite content, left the youngest in the possession of the throne, saying that a hundred kings could not reign in one country, and that, if they tried, it would be for the woe of the people.

"So all the brothers went back to their own in peace and amity."

When the King of Ava read the priest's letter, he was so well pleased with the narrative that he sent a messenger to him, and appointed him head of the ecclesiastical body, with a residence near the palace.

THE COMMAND OF THE KING.

THERE was a King of Amarapoora, who reigned in a time long past.

He was young and beloved, and fair of form and face, and his people lived but to obey his lightest wish. He dwelt in a palace of crystal, surrounded by gardens, of whose beauty no tongue could tell. He had money and lands and gems, and beautiful wives and unnumbered treasures, gathered from all lands.

He could have whatsoever he willed, and go wheresoever he listed. His days and nights were one long dream of gladness.

No enemies plagued him; no troubles of any sort visited him; his coffers were well filled, and his ministers were faithful and wise; and yet, in spite of all, he was weary of everything, more weary than he could say.

He drank from a goblet of gold, rimmed with a band of pearls, and his clothes were studded with rubies and emeralds; he was flattered and courted and envied as no monarch had ever been envied before, and he was more discontented than the poorest subject in his realms.

Above and around and about him was all that is most conducive to happiness, but within him were fatigue and desolation.

All that he had ever wished for had been given unto him; never had the gods left unanswered his prayers; other and better men's they turned a deaf ear to, but not so this King's, and now he had nothing more left to crave for.

He had supreme power vested in his hands, but he was indifferent to it; he owned everything that the heart could desire, and those very possessions were killing him.

For the trail of the serpent of satiety lay over his garden of Eden.

Never had his eyes rested on disease or want or poverty, or anything that could distress his mind.

All gifts and graces had been showered upon him; his sins were buried in oblivion, or cited more admiringly than the virtues of others.

When he went abroad on his white elephant, with its trappings of scarlet and silver, the very air was perfumed with otto of rose, while the people bowed and kissed the dust through which he passed.

Attached to the palace were many hundreds of officials, players, dancers, jugglers, and clowns; for the King sought only one thing, and that was—Amusement; of which, in no matter what form it was presented to him, he soon tired.

Constantly was the country being searched for some one with a ready wit, an inventive tongue, or a nimble foot, to pass the hours for the Lord of the City of Gems.

Tellers of marvellous stories, more wonderful than the Arabian Nights, had come, and tried their little best to please.

There were those who travelled specially to other countries, but to return and tell him of all that they had seen, and of how inferior all lands and rulers were when compared with their own.

Dancing women, with the classic limbs and straight black brows of Egypt, sought his favour.

Eyes that were as loadstars in their brilliancy wooed him with a thousand glances.

Circassian women, with sun-flecked tresses, were his willing slaves.

Men of great learning asked nothing better than to gain his ear awhile, but all fatigued him soon.

And, like a child, he cried for something new.

Then one day a stranger from India presented himself at the great gates of the palace, saying that he brought a game called Chess to teach the King. They who loitered round the entrance bade him scornfully to "begone." What would he of the Golden Feet do with red and white figures like that? they contemptuously asked.

But the Indian protested, craving humbly to be granted an audience. Then one, who was more kindly than the rest, led him through the green, silent gardens, with their aisles of gorgeous roses; by spray-splashing fountains, fringed with the lotus-flower; up a flight of marble steps on to a terrace where peacocks strolled; through carved doors, from which stretched an endless vista of halls and rooms filled with numerous attendants, who formed a mass of marvellous colour; carpets and rugs of velvet-like softness were strewn about; ivory of wonderful workmanship; things of all precious metals, together with stuffs of delicate hues and lovely texture; to a chamber handsomer than any that had gone before, where at one end, seated on a couch, clad in an odd, rich fashion, and shaded by a large umbrella, was the King, his bare feet resting on a stool; to his right was a golden spittoon, while to his left stood a slave holding a jewelled betel box and some green cigars.

The Burmese prostrated himself almost full length, motioning the Indian to do likewise, explaining at the same time the object of their presence.

His royal master received them graciously, inquired into the merits of the game, finally declaring that he would be taught it there and then.

From that time forth he devoted himself to play with an eagerness entirely foreign to his nature. He paused for nothing, never going without the palace. The days seemed not half long enough. The courtiers were inclined to congratulate themselves on having at last found something that seemed likely to continue a favourite with the King, until they saw how high the Indian was rising in his favour, being loaded with money and presents, and thereby becoming a cause of bitter envy and jealousy on the part of the Burmese ministers.

Nor did his haughty, overbearing manner tend to soften their resentment. Many were the plans that they made to cause his downfall, but in vain. Every one of the plots failed, while he whom they conspired against seemed to grow but dearer to the Lord of the Rising Sun.

Time passed.

Then one came called Nicomar from a great distance, who brought painted cards and dice wherewith to amuse the monarch, the like of which had never been seen before. And the King, like a spoilt baby, was delighted with this new toy, and thrust away the chess from his sight with disdain.

And those round about were so glad of the change that they hardly grudged the new-comer the honours that their royal master began to speedily heap upon him.

The days went by, and His Majesty did nothing but recline on his crimson and golden cushions, playing and rattling the dice-box.

Then, after awhile, he took to enlivening the game by hazarding large bets with his teacher—bets which generally meant the performance of impossible feats by Nicomar, with many penalties attached to their non-accomplishment.

Often and sorely was Nicomar's subtle mind perplexed to devise means of circumventing his master's wagers, and of distracting his attention to other and more entertaining matters. Nicomar lived always in fear of losing his place at the palace. Inwardly, he hated this unreasoning and unreasonable monarch, whom nothing pleased for long; outwardly, he was the most docile, obedient, and fawning of servants.

Carefully did he veil his night-like eyes, lest the hatred that shone in them sometimes might be read by those around.

Prostrate before the King, he seemingly lived but for his smile.

The burning days and the sultry nights he devoted to his service; while others slept he sat wakeful, thinking out new forms of amusement, new ways to distract the King, and enable him to retain that place which to him, hitherto most poor and friendless, was as the sorcerer's golden apple.

For Nicomar there was but one god—and that god was wealth.

He laboured and strove for and endlessly desired it.

A year went by, and still he remained the favourite, and he began to feel a little more secure and at ease....

"Nicomar," cried the King one day, as they sat together in the sunset glow, "I have resolved that you shall put milk where the sea now is. I have tired of water, and I desire instead an ocean of milk."

Nicomar stared in dismay.

"That which your Majesty wishes is impossible," he made answer.

The King frowned.

"Impossible is no word between you and me. That which I command must never be impossible," he exclaimed angrily. "Hitherto you have obeyed my orders; do so now."

The Indian trembled, but dared not protest.

"Fill up the sea with milk in fourteen days from now and your reward shall be all that even you can desire;—fail to do so and you shall die by all the tortures possible within an hour. Do as I say and your place shall be the very highest here: your power shall be well-nigh limitless, your name shall be on all lips; men shall crouch at your feet; you shall have a finer palace and greater wealth than any in the land. Save myself, you shall be great and free, while those whom you love shall be raised also."

Nicomar salaamed silently.

The King continued:

"You have known what it is to be lowly and despised; you have been mocked and reviled at,—what greater or sweeter vengeance then to see those very people bow down before you your slaves? I desire this thing so much that any price you like to name I am prepared to give."

The Indian answered never a word.

He knew of old that once the King commanded it was useless to do aught but comply.

This reward, great as it was, could never be his, for to earn it was beyond anybody's power.

"Begone, now," continued His Majesty, "and return in fourteen days' time to claim your prize, or——" and his gesture was more eloquent than words.

Nicomar, with sorrowful, halting gait, went from his august presence.

He sought without delay the quietude of his own rooms. He was well-nigh distracted. From many difficult predicaments he had with consummate tact and skill extricated himself, but from this there seemed no escape.

He beat his breast and tore his hair. He consulted the wise men and the stars; looked for this sign and for that; prayed long and fervently, and propitiated the gods in many ways, but all to no purpose.

He took no food or rest; he dared not think of what awaited him in the near future.

So a week went by, and he was no nearer finding a loophole through which to escape.

On the seventh day he sought the King, and craved humbly to know if he had understood him aright, or had he been but jesting with him.

He lingered but a short while in doubt.

His Majesty was deeply incensed at being questioned, and let the full torrent of his displeasure fall upon the head of his luckless servitor.

Swearing many oaths by the sacred hairs of Buddha that his will should be obeyed, he had him thrust ignominiously from his presence.

Then Nicomar went from out the palace and the city far into the lonely country, seeking he knew not what. For days he wandered wearily through thick jungle and silent forest ways, stepping but slowly in the long, dank grass.

He suffered greatly, and suffered without hope.

On the fifth day he came to where a broad river flowed and sparkled between high green banks.

Some Burmese, driving bullocks, were resting beside it, while in the distance were a few mud huts.

Nicomar, who was footsore and faint, sank down at the foot of a banana tree.

His garments were torn by branches and brambles, his sight was blinded by the sun, his mouth parched with thirst.

Idly he watched the Burmese from where he sat.

Soon it became apparent that they desired to cross that glittering expanse of water, but evidently knew not how to accomplish it.

Nicomar, tired of thinking of his own miseries, grew unconsciously interested.

Three of them twisted their silk pasohs up about their waists, and tried to wade the river; but it was too deep, and they returned, seemingly much perplexed.

Then they consulted together; whereupon one among them—evidently against the desire of his companions, as their gestures betokened—took the rope of his bullock between his teeth, and diving into the river, with a good imitation of swimming reached the other side.

His fellows watched the performance with open-eyed wonder, but could not be induced to follow his example.

Nicomar, looking on, thought that the young man must have a mind full of resource, and so determined to seek him and consult with him. He could not have told what was exactly the impulse that urged him to this course, but he rose, and staggering a little because he was faint, made his way to the river bank.

The young fellow leant a very interested and attentive ear to the strange story that Nicomar told to him. When he had finished he took him to his hut and gave him a meal of rice, then bade him go over the tale once more in all its details.

Whereupon he asked at the conclusion—

"If I, poor and ignorant, satisfy the King that his command can be performed, what will you give unto me?"

Nicomar, trembling with joy and incredulity, promised him one half of what he had and the hand of his daughter in marriage.

Then the Burman said—

"To-morrow we will seek the King." More he would not say, but sat in the dusky gloom of the coming evening, smoking.

Nicomar, with the great weight of his troubles somewhat lightened, slept heavily.

On the morning of the fourteenth day Nicomar prostrated himself before his master.

"Well," asked the King, "come you to claim your reward?"

The Indian bowed his head in grave deferential assent.

"And so you have obeyed my order?"

"I but wait for your Majesty to perform your part first, then I will without delay do my share."

The King hastened to ask the meaning of such an answer.

"Your Majesty commanded me," replied the Indian, "to fill up the sea with milk, which I am quite ready to do; but your Majesty did not command me to take the water from the ocean, and until that is done it is impossible to fill it anew. If your Majesty," continued Nicomar, "will but dispose of the water ——." Then he paused timidly, waiting the King's response. He had done as the Burman had instructed him, and he feared the result.

For a long while there was silence, and those round about trembled with apprehension, for they guessed not in what wise their master would take such a reply.

At last he smiled, for although he had many grave faults, he was not unkindly or averse to owning himself baffled.

Then he said—

"Nicomar, thou art cleverer than I thought."

At which words hearts that had stood still from fear beat once more.

"The sea exists," said his Majesty, after a pause, looking round on his Court, "as it existed before we were, as it will exist when we have all passed away and our names have been forgotten."

Also Available from JiaHu Books

The Discovery of the Source of the Nile – Speke – 9781909669550

A Burmese Reader - Annotated Selections from the Sudhammacari - Rev. Andrew St. John – 9781909669086

An English Girl's First Impressions of Burmah – Beth Ellis - 9781784350604

www.ingramcontent.com/pod-product-compliance
Lightning Source LLC
Chambersburg PA
CBHW031428040426
42444CB00006B/742